What People Are Saying About

Pagan Portals - Venezuelan Folklore

A delightfully compact digest of Aesopian-esque legends and lore from the often overlooked, yet mystically potent, culture of Venezuela as shared by a local with a unique view into Latin American magic.

Tomás Prower author of *La Santa Muerte: Unearthing the Magic and Mysticism of Death*

Venezuelan Folklore: Spirits and Legends of the Dead, written by Alan U. Dalul, may be short in length, but it undeniably takes readers on a captivating journey into the realm of Venezuelan folklore. Through a clear and succinct storytelling approach, Dalul transports readers into a world teeming with spirits, legends, and vibrant cultural traditions. This book is a must-read for anyone intrigued by the spirits and legends that shape the country's rich cultural heritage.

Lawren Leo, author of *Dragonflame* and *Horse Magick*

Pagan Portals
Venezuelan Folklore

Pagan Portals
Venezuelan Folklore

Spirits and Legends of the Dead

Alan U. Dalul

MOON BOOKS

London, UK
Washington, DC, USA

CollectiveInk

First published by Moon Books, 2024
Moon Books is an imprint of Collective Ink Ltd.,
Unit 11, Shepperton House, 89 Shepperton Road, London, N1 3DF
office@collectiveinkbooks.com
www.collectiveinkbooks.com
www.moon-books.net

For distributor details and how to order please visit the 'Ordering' section on our website.

ISBN: 978 1 80341 544 4
978 1 80341 571 0 (ebook)
Library of Congress Control Number: 2023937224

A CIP catalogue record for this book is available from the British Library.

Design: Lapiz Digital Services

UK: Printed and bound by CPI Group (UK) Ltd, Croydon, CR0 4YY
Printed in North America by CPI GPS partners

We operate a distinctive and ethical publishing philosophy in all areas of our business, from our global network of authors to production and worldwide distribution.

Contents

Introduction

When you think about Latin American folklore, what comes to mind? Mexican Día de los Muertos? Maybe that horror movie about La Llorona? Stories about Curanderismo? Maybe. And maybe you think that's it. I can't blame you. It was the same for me.

I didn't see any kind of Venezuelan representation as I grew up. I never saw an arepa in the shows I liked, heard a gaita, or saw El Lago de Maracaibo in a movie. I didn't care either. I didn't feel like I belonged there, didn't identify with the culture, so I found a place among fantasy and horror novels, metal music, K-pop, anime, European Folklore, some customs from my Syrian family, but I even went on to say "Venezuela hasn't done anything for me".

I was full of anger, full of resentment, frustrated, and lost. Most of all, I was wrong.

After a long series of events, my family and I had to leave. We had to start from scratch because staying there wasn't safe. More than once our lives were in danger in Venezuela, our opportunities were lacking, less with every passing day, same as with the quality.

The life my grandparents and parents had built was crumbling in front of our very eyes. I lost my dad in the middle of all that due to an uncontrollable cancer, and I couldn't stop thinking "if we were not in Venezuela, he would still be alive".

I had to study a remote Master's degree in the middle of unpredictable blackouts that would last for 10 hours, or more, every day with a deficient laptop that could hardly function. My mom had to abandon her studies for the millionth time so she could sustain my brother and I. My brother spent entire days waiting at gas stations despite his diabetes just for the National

1

Guard to come and say "this is just for those who support the government".

The times I was part of the protests and fought for a change, while still a student, people threw stones at me, and someone even tried to cut me in the stomach. Had it not been for a friend I had at the time that pushed me and told me "get back! get back!" a government sympathizer, a *chavista*, would have killed me. They tried to hurt me again years later, as a journalist, almost hitting me in the head and trying to make me and the bike rider taking me to the office fall. I don't need to imagine what they would have done to us.

It was as if I was trapped in a big jail where the people in charge were hunting down whoever opposed them. A lot of people "*creen que tienen a Dios agarrado por las bolas*," think they have "God by the balls", as we Venezuelans say, meaning they think they have the right to do as they please.

Just because they have a uniform and a title they think they can do whatever they want.

When I said I wanted to be a writer, people mocked me, they thought I was weird, crazy, and very few believed in me. When they knew I wanted to write fantasy and would rather stay at home reading about vampires and witches instead of play sports, drink beer, have casual sex with strangers in a cheap motel, and dance reggaeton, I was told I was boring. I hated the whole country and took pride in it.

However, a few years ago I started writing about that same country for The Wild Hunt, discovering its legends, its spirits, its own kind of magic. There was a whole universe filled with specters and morals waiting for me in the oral tradition, tales that parents and grandparents have told their kids for generations. I knew two or three from my childhood, but I never thought there would be so many.

Month after month, I discovered a new being, each with its own stories, teachings, and charm. Month after month, I would send my editor a new piece and feel excited about that pantheon of sorts I was discovering. Years passed me by, and I didn't notice.

I never saw myself as part of Venezuela, and didn't want to be, either, until I was far away and found a home in its ghosts. I still like metal, rock, and K-pop music, still like bands and artists my family doesn't know about, still love sushi, and want to spend my days with books, tarot decks, and live close to a forest in cold weather. However, I would never change an arepa or my grandma's hallacas (and she's Syrian!) for any of those. I miss those holidays with my family with Zulian Gaita in the background as my cousins and I joked and spoke about anime.

I wanted to escape from Zulia and its inclement sun, that eternal hot weather I had to endure day after day when the electricity failed for hours and even days. I wanted to escape from the bad memories, the trauma, the danger, the constant worry that something would happen to me or my family, the fear that we could be killed in bright daylight. I wanted to escape like my father and my grandparents escaped the Syrian wat and dictatorship. I never took pride in my Venezuelan heritage. Until I started missing Venezuela.

This book is the result of all those years discovering the legends from the land I grew up in. It's the story of how I discovered magic in the hot streets of Maracaibo, the mysteries in my own Syrian family, how a folk saint saved one of my cousins, how my father protected my brother and me in the darkest nights.

While it is true that I am Venezuelan and wrote about indigenous legends and myths now and then, I realized that I didn't want to include something that does not belong to me. La Llorona, El Silbón, La Loca Luz Caraballo, María Lionza... They are all well-known in Venezuela, but indigenous people have been seen as inferior and mocked for staying loyal to their roots from the beginning.

It's one thing to show their world in a monthly column, but it's a completely different thing to feel as if it is my right to tell their stories in a more permanent way and get paid for that. It is not my job to show their culture, I cannot tell the legends I discovered as I wrote those columns, it doesn't feel right, but I do, can and will share the ones I grew up with. And it is my hope that readers will get interested in legends such as El Dueño del Fuego, Carú, Caribay, and many more.

I'm a believer that legends and folklore are a big repertoire of inspiration and reference for a Witch's craft and spirituality. Because of that, I'm including several journaling prompts so readers from different backgrounds can dwell on the themes of each story regardless of their cultural background.

These spirits are Venezuelan, and the topics they speak about are universal, but some stories change in different parts of Latin America, so I'm sticking to the versions I heard as a child, or that my friends shared with me. I'm including a few chapters that, while not related to folklore, speak about a practice influenced by my experiences and limitations as a Witch living in Venezuela. You can say it's my personal folklore.

Without realizing it, I learned to love these legends and their symbolism. They started the process of embracing my roots, honoring them, respecting them, because even though my family is Syrian, we were born and raised in Venezuela, a country just as imperfect as any other but a rich folklore, a land and people who refuse to be defined by a national crisis, a tyrannical government, and a conservative society, but that is also a place inhabited by endless spirits that fill with mystery, fantasy, and magic.

Honoring My Ancestors without Visiting Their Tombs

I find much to admire in the past; it always has something more to say, something more to teach us, something more to be discovered within it. Mine in particular intrigues me constantly. This attraction includes my ancestors, especially those related by blood. I remember them through seeing their photos, recalling the good times at their side and their voices. If I didn't know them, I imagine what their lives were like and the stories I've heard about them, which also includes asking questions whenever I can.

Although I differ in many things with my family, I share their respect towards the deceased. All my ancestors, however, are either in a graveyard that is being assaulted and robbed, and so the air in it is putrid, or they were buried in another country.

The cemetery in my hometown has become highly insecure as a result of the frequent presence of thieves, kidnappers, and other criminals, while the graves of the dead are violated to steal the organs of the recently deceased and sell them, or to steal their bones and use them in various rituals (which I find highly disrespectful). Not only I couldn't go there while I was in Venezuela, but it's also impossible for me to visit them in other countries, go to the other side of the globe. Chances are I will not do it for a while.

Despite these conditions, I found different, simple, and effective ways to keep the tradition alive and honor their memory. I might not be the most rigorous in terms of devotion, but I'm honest, attentive, and try to do better every time.

Talking to Them: In my home in Maracaibo there are several photos of my ancestors – not all of them, but many, and it's the same in my relatives' houses. Whenever I felt the need to get near my ancestors, to reconnect with them, maybe to learn something about them, maybe because of yearning for them, I would get a photo and mentally talk to them. I try not to follow any protocol, so it's a natural process, a conversation like when they were alive. Although I don't always get an answer, the connection is very therapeutic and it helps me remember I am not alone. Even just looking at their photos gives me peace.

Water Offerings to the Family Tree: I once sat down with my maternal grandma and asked her if she could give me the names of the ancestors: her parents, her grandparents, those from my paternal side, and so on. I ended up with an incomplete tree, lacking aunts, uncles, cousins, and maybe even some marriages, but it was a start. Every time I can, I leave an offering of water in front of it and bless my ancestors. It's something I did in Venezuela and, when I left, that tree was one of the first things I took with me. I still have to this day.

Candle Offerings: Lighting candles is very common in my family. They mark promises, petitions, even house blessings, or religious dates. I light them when I thank my ancestors or ask them for help, usually along with the water offerings. In Venezuela, I burned the end of the candle so it wouldn't move from the plate I used, lit the wick and thought about the face and name of my ancestor. If I needed their help, I asked for it after that, and if that wasn't the case, I asked the universe to send them the candle's light. If, on the contrary, I receive a message without asking, I do it in acknowledgement. Now I just light candles in front of my tree, sometimes I miss a day or more, but I always think of them during my day.

Speaking Their Names: When I have the basic information – the whole name, dates of birth and death – of someone I want to honor, I write it on paper, pronounce it in a low voice or repeat the information in my mind. I get comfortable, close my eyes, and use their name and dates as a mantra. I try to work while the place is in silence. I say my goodbyes aloud if I have already spoken. If I wrote something down, I erase or dispose of the paper. A more recent practice is reciting their names from the closest one, which is my dad, and following a line through the tree, all of them in order, until I reach the last one I am aware of. It gives me a peace I can't describe. It also reminds me that I'm protected and blessed.

Listening to Music: I'm not speaking about the music they listened to, but songs that make me remember my ancestors, tracks that for some reason I connect with a particular relative. I simply put on my headphones, turn up the volume and sing along in my mind with the song, envisioning the face or faces I start to remember. The music I listen to always becomes connected with many feelings, memories, and ideas. Whatever I do, I always do it better with music, and it all becomes an emotional process. I'm not ashamed of saying it makes me cry sometimes, especially when it's a song that reminds me of my dad. It's also interesting to notice what kind of songs you use, what that common thread could tell you.

Keeping Belongings and Mementos: I have my paternal grandfather's glasses and used to have a piece of wood from my dad's studio, which I left in Venezuela, but I have two of his watches, and my brother has one as well. Those are physical reminders, objects that either belonged to my ancestors or remind me of them in some way. Just taking them, seeing them and remembering the energy they keep makes me feel they are with me, that there's a part of them that remains in this plane by my side. I do not worship them, I know they are objects, but it's the connection, the emotional value they carry, that makes them so powerful to me.

There are more methods, but these are the ones I use and connect me with my roots the most. They help me cross the line between life and death, remember my lineage, where I come from, and that one (hopefully very distant) day, I will be an ancestor as well. No matter the ups and downs in my relationship with the dead, or even if I didn't get to know them, I have a special place in my heart reserved for those who passed away.

Journaling Prompts

- What would you do if you couldn't visit your ancestors in the cemetery?
- Do you have a place for them in your home, or room, or prayers?
- Do you acknowledge them in any way?
- Do you have a family tree? If so, how do you feel when you look at it? If not, do you feel the need for one?
- What family relics do you have at home, if any? Which do you think your descendants could have to remember you?

Prayers for Walking Late at Night

Living in a country like Venezuela, which is more unstable with every year, has made me think that anything could happen to me at any time – particularly during the night, when anyone could come close to me and I wouldn't realize. I never gave it any previous thought until, one night, I had to go to the supermarket. The street was so desolate that I thought to myself, "I could be murdered and no one would know until the morning."

The words got out of my mouth before I could process them: *"En sombras habito y en sombras camino, en sobras aguardo y en sombras me resguardo."* An English version with the same feeling, although not literal, would be: "In shadows I live and in shadows I walk, in shadows I wait, in shadows I won't fall."

Call it a prayer, an affirmation, a spell, an incantation, or whatever suits your spiritual path. The name doesn't matter, but the effect does. I used it many times and safely did whatever I had to do, walking alone at night.

Darkness doesn't represent evil to me, just the unseen, that which we fear, that which we are still unable to control. If we go back to any creation myth, it all starts with darkness, with an emptiness that would then be filled, and it will always end in darkness as well.

Darkness is original, it's a primal element, it's the alpha and the omega of everything there was, there is and there will be. Darkness is timeless, it doesn't understand limits such as time and space. Rather than look at it as the enemy, I work with it as my sidekick and, therefore, when practicing divination, I take refuge in darkness and ask for its guidance.

While it is true that it's harder and requires a lot of care and patience, working with darkness as tarot is concerned has given me good results. I have discovered that dark decks say what we

9

need to know instead of what we *want* to know. Darkness gives you what you need.

After that first night, something clicked in me. I usually had to go out at night to buy this or that at the supermarket we had on the next corner, and it wasn't a long walk, just a couple of minutes to arrive, but it only takes seconds to end a life. Why take a risk if I could have support instead? Some could say that this is just psychological, that it's the law of attraction, but it has worked again and again and again regardless of the reason. The name for the practice, again, is unimportant.

One doesn't have to live in an unstable country, such as Venezuela, to ask Darkness for protection and shelter. If someone needs it, finds comfort, beauty, or both in it, and understands that it doesn't equal evil or harm, nor is it necessarily negative in any sense, then feel free to speak to Darkness, honestly. Just be clear and concise.

These rhymes are just my approach on the matter. I feel better when my words rhyme. But one certainly doesn't have to be a poet to ask for help. However, if you find rhymes appealing and feel more comfortable including them, then try using one of these options – or use them all – as a whole prayer or spell, or as a basis to create an entirely different thing. Do what feels most comfortable.

Sombras y las tinieblas a mi alrededor, protejan este corazón de daño y maldad.
(Deidad de tu preferencia), ven a mí en esta noche de necesidad.
Ningún daño vendrá en mi camino, iré y vendré sin pavor ni suplicio.
Luna plateada en lo alto, permíteme llegar a casa sano y salvo.

Shadows and darkness that surround me, protect from harm this noble heart.
[Deity of preference], come to me in this night of need.

No harm shall come my way, I shall be safe from harm and
pain.
Silver moon in the sky, protect me as I walk/let me come
back home safe and sound.

Journaling Prompts

- How do you feel when there's no light?
- What does darkness mean for you?
- Are you comfortable at night?
- What goes through your mind when there's silence and
darkness all around?

Spontaneous Prayers and Incantations

I consider myself a fairly methodical, structured, and orderly person. Everything I do must have an order shaped by specific steps, particularly when it comes to my spirituality, which is when I decide to be more organized. There's a chance I *might* have autism, or some other mental condition, so that *might* be the reason why. However, there's a time when you have to forget structure and simply follow what your intuition dictates.

With the passage of time, I formed my own spiritual practices, learning as much as I can from different cultures, trying to keep myself both correct and true to their origins and to myself. I described myself as an eclectic Witch, and by that I meant that I took a little of everything, what I consider correct and necessary, but always staying respectful toward the source without appropriating anything, and creating a personal practice. I still use that term now and then for the sake of simplicity, but my practice has changed from that approach.

Some parts of my practice remained static for a long time, but they all changed, some with more ease than others. I modified and discharged as I saw fit, such as meditations, my way of connecting with the divine energy and understanding it, especially the prayers and incantations I use.

There are times when I don't have my notes, my ideas or anything at hand. There's no way to review what I've done before, like when, on a typical day, I'm on public transport and feel something isn't right.

I believe that all living beings have energy, including inanimate ones, and that it's possible to give it form and purpose to manifest changes. Humans are not the exception to this, so if the need appears, it doesn't seem right or ethical to do nothing, except on very rare occasions.

Considering that first example, I simply identify *what* bothers or worries me, and I verbalize it in my mind, followed by my desire and its possible solution. Simple, direct, and (until now) effective. It is a method that's always worked for me, one that I use whenever necessary.

You don't have to say everything out loud, or say it in words. I certainly don't do it like that all the time. I usually close my eyes, take a breath, forget my surroundings and, suddenly, it's just me and my thoughts, directed like an arrow straight to my desire, my goal, that prayer or that incantation.

For me, a prayer is an interaction with divine energy, or, as I say, "the people from above." God, Goddess, Buddha, Odin, virgins, angels, guardians, ancestors, Gods, the universe... names abound, but the essence is the same in general terms: a divine force that might be one or several. No matter what we call it, what face or characteristics we give it, the idea is present in different societies and cultures.

A prayer is usually understood as a way of asking for help, asking for assistance and intervention when the situation warrants it. You can also pray to say thank you and show appreciation, but let's stay with the request part for now to keep it simple.

An incantation, on the contrary, is the manifestation of our will, our personal energy, formed and directed towards a specific objective using the verbal or mental word, optionally with the help of other materials or energies.

When I started learning Witchcraft, I learned that since we were created by the Gods, then there's something divine in all of us, and so I understood incantations as our voice using that divine spark. You could say that this is the most basic form of magic: recognizing the divine inside.

Many cultures have used both, and each technique carries power with it. The power of tradition, repetition, and antiquity is undeniable. They are proven formulas and methods that have been passed down for generations because they're useful. However, traditions began as innovations as well.

Sometimes, situations force us to think outside the box, leave our comfort zone, and this applies to any aspect of life. Innovating is not about forgetting our customs and traditions, but about creating a new one and allowing those that exist, those in which we trust, evolve over time.

A static spiritual practice can be depressing and boring to some, and could lead to failure if it against common sense and inclusion, even more if we're talking about a shared practice that welcomes others into it.

You could also run the risk of it becoming a chore to be done with. I don't think it's always right to keep doing exactly the same thing over and over again. Allowing rituals and ideas to grow is an important part of my spirituality, always keeping a small window for new things, new approaches, intuition, and inspiration. This not only re-enlivens our practice. It offers a new perspective, vivifies it, keeps it new, full of mysteries, expectations, promises. The day our faith stagnates, it will have failed.

Although I'm still learning to trust my intuition, learning to identify when it is my faith that speaks, and when it is my overthinking head, it becomes easier every day to let everything flow and nothing to influence. Sometimes faith must be like a river, and the believer a swimmer. Sometimes we have to trust the current will take us to a good port, and modify the way we swim. So far, it hasn't failed me.

Journaling Prompts

- When was the last time you practiced your spirituality or religion without a fixed script?
- Do you understand the reasons and meanings behind what you do in your practice? Does it make sense to you?
- Is it comfortable for you to do something spontaneous? Do you like the idea? Why?

El Silbón: A Legend About (Problematic) Ancestors

The legend of El Silbón (The Whistler) is one of the most popular in Latin America, a family tragedy whose reality has been lost in time. The story that surrounds this specter changes a little depending on the country in which it is told, but no matter what, it causes nightmares for any child. That was the case for me when I read it in elementary school. Although I have always felt a lot of interest in the myths, legends, and fables of many cultures, the Greek more than any other, few legends have made such an impression on me as that of El Silbón.

It is said that in the Venezuelan Llanos, there once lived a young boy who worked every day to help his family. He lived with his parents and his paternal grandfather, who were strict with him because they wished him to be noble of heart.

One day, while returning from work, his father, a violent man, accused his wife of being unfaithful. The discussion went out of control and ended with the mother's death. Enraged, the young man disemboweled his father in revenge, but this wasn't the end of it.

When his paternal grandfather learned everything that happened, he made the young man be tied to a pole in the middle of the field and whipped him until his back was shattered. After washing his wounds with brandy, he released him, along with two hungry, rabid dogs to pursue him. As the young man walked away, the grandfather cursed him, condemning him to carry his father's bones forever.

Since then, El Silbón walks through Los Llanos, carrying his father's bones in a sack on his back. They say that his characteristic whistle announces his presence: when heard nearby, El Silbón is far away, but if it seems to be distant, then the specter is close.

There are several versions of El Silbón and its effect on people. Some say that he appears to bad men, whom he murders mercilessly with a machete; others say he comes to announce a death in the family when he arrives at a house, where he begins to count his father's bones during the night. Everything will be fine if no one hears him, but if someone does, that person will die before the morning.

Few things repel El Silbón, but the most popular protections are the barking of a dog, a whip, and the Lord's Prayer, which is said to scare the specter in the act. Rereading the legend, I think that alcohol could act as a defense, especially brandy.

This sort of Latin male banshee has attracted the attention of many and is used as a warning to irresponsible men and womanizers, but I think one aspect of it hasn't been given its due importance: the ancestors and heritage, especially problematic ancestors, and transgenerational trauma. When we remember our ancestors, both those of blood and those who are not, are we aware that they also made mistakes when they lived? We almost always idealize the deceased, seeking to have a good memory instead of a real one. Nobody wants to speak ill of the dead, but out of respect for ourselves and them, it's best to always recognize them as the human beings they were, with both good qualities and defects.

The legend of El Silbón always makes me think that our ancestors made mistakes, but that many times it is not up to us to remedy them. In any case, if we must do it, we must heal and bless, not act driven by violence and revenge.

How many times have we stopped to think that, despite their mistakes, our ancestors want to see us well and blessed? And I mean really being aware that their love for us is immense. Death does not change mortals but frees them from the limited vision of being human. I've seen that happen in my family.

Being a Witch has made me see that the blessing of my ancestors is sacred, that one's lineage is the greatest gift. Where would we be today if not for them? Like it or not, we owe them life. Walking, breathing, being able to see, being here at this precise moment, all of this is thanks to them. If you ask me, we should always remember them, tell their stories, and learn from the mistakes of our ancestors.

When it comes to toxic ancestors, relatives that left trauma behind them, there's no obligation to honor them. I think we should still remember them and learn from their mistakes, work on healing ourselves and, if possible, heal those affected by them. We have total freedom not to work with them, and if the only healing comes from erasing their names from the family tree, as I know some have done, as much as it makes me uncomfortable and as much as I dislike the idea, then it could be an option some might night to ponder. It's not my place to say if it's right or wrong. Do what works. But always, always, remember where you come from so you can try to do better than those who came before.

Journaling Prompts

- Which word would you choose to describe El Silbón's story? Why did you choose it?
- How was your relationship with your father? If you didn't have one, what about a paternal figure? What positive and negative memories do you have? What can you learn from them?
- How do you feel about your ancestors?

La Llorona: The Venezuelan Banshee?

This may be the most famous Latin myth ever. The figure of La Llorona (The Crying Woman, or The Wailer) is one of those legends that's hard to forget once you learn about it. As tends to happen, her story changes depending on time and space, but the moral remains the same: holding on to the past is nothing but a death sentence. I discovered this specter when I was a boy. I no longer remember if I read it or heard it, but the story has stayed unaltered in my memory since then, no matter how many versions I discover later.

Long ago, a woman whose name was lost in the wind became pregnant by a man whose identity was also erased. From them, two boys were born, little ones that lost their father when he decided to leave for no apparent reason. The mother, left to her own luck, loathed the chain imposed on her, so she forgot any responsibility toward the fruits of her womb.

At first, she forgot just once in a while, and then it was every night. The hours passed while she danced with other men until the sun came back and her children were left alone in the darkness of their icy home. It seemed that everything would be alright, until an unattended candle provoked an infernal fire.

The mother was the last one to know and the last to arrive. Her heart shattered, now aware of what she had done, she threw herself to the ground, consumed by her own flames and shrieks, as her home burned before her eyes. The neighbors that in vain tried to save the little creatures paid their fury against her. She offered no resistance, hoping to be reunited with her darlings.

But this wasn't meant to be. From her grave her spirit rose, damned by her mistakes, unable to find any rest. Blinded by pain, La Llorona haunts the roads, searching for her sons, finding them in every child that crosses her path, and taking them from the living.

The legend always resonated in my mind when I remembered it because I felt just like that, a creature full of pain, full of sadness and desperation, unable to move, but that doesn't mean I couldn't really move. I searched for healing everywhere I could and if something didn't work then I'd try again with something different. La Llorona taught me it's easy to let ourselves be defeated, that it's a matter of closing one's eyes and letting the stones rain down, but the price is too high.

They say that going through a traumatic event makes you sensible, it makes your hidden gifts go up to the surface. After years of bullying, abuse, harm from my classmates, and even from people I thought would be there with me, after a relationship that made me look at the abyss once again, I realized it was true.

Traumas turned into my impulse, pain a language I became an expert in, and memories turned into an endless pool of ideas. My time in the shadows made me strong, and I was able to notice this in time. The secret was just breathing in and trusting. Trusting in time, my guides, my masters, my ancestors, my heroes, all my personal pantheon, and maybe something else I don't know how to name. I still cry, but unlike La Llorona, I'm not a prisoner of my tears anymore.

Journal Prompts

- What makes you cry? Do you know why?
- Is there anything you haven't forgiven yourself for?
- How do you react when someone makes a great mistake?
- What's the first thing that comes to mind when you read "depression"? Don't analyze it. Just write non-stop to see where you go. What can you learn from that?

La Sayona: Revenge, Treason, and Motherhood

Some legends go down in history. Others are forgotten. And only some, exceptional cases, live in a liminal space, known only to a few. Long ago I heard the story of La Sayona, which could be translated as "The Sackcloth-Woman", a specter that inhabits the Venezuelan Llanos and punishes cheating men. Her legend is one of these exceptions.

In the version I learned as a kid, a woman lived happily married to her husband, a hard-working and honest man who had given her a son. The couple lived without any problem, the man worked and the woman took care of the home, and both were content to carry their day to day like this.

On one occasion, however, a rumor reached the woman's ears, stating that her husband had an affair with her mother. It was just that, just a rumor, nothing more, nothing less, but she still went to her mother's home. Upon arriving, she found her husband asleep there, with a baby in his arms. Enraged, the woman killed her husband and mother, but before dying, her mother cursed her, condemning her to wander the plains punishing unfaithful men.

Some versions say that the woman's name was Casilda, and that she set fire to her mother's house, where her husband and baby were, and then killed her mother with a machete, opening her belly. Others say that this specter can shape-shift, presenting herself as a dog, a wolf, or a woman with long black hair, dressed in a cloak of the same color. Finally, it has also been said that La Sayona gives a cry that bristles the skin.

Taking justice into our hands is too tempting, and though I'm sure more than one has done it, each experience being different, all such acts have one thing in common: when acting under the influence of anger, the remedy is worse than the evil that afflicts.

This legend reminds me a lot of that of El Silbón, where punishing someone else when it is not our responsibility ends in a worse sentence than we imagined, but there's a key element here: betrayal. It is true that trust is built over the years and is lost in just a second, with just one mistake, but gossip is the worst enemy that can exist for her.

From the moment she was cursed by her mother, La Sayona is said to punish unfaithful men and those who are willing to be, either by scaring them or by eating their bodies with animal fangs she reveals when it is too late. We could say that she's an avenger of the marriage bond, a feminine force of justice, but we would be leaving aside the fact that, in her anger, her desire for revenge, she lost the possibility of any rest. All her energy and power are used just for punishment.

It's very easy to get carried away by anger, but it's expensive to repair the damage, and sometimes it's not even possible, as in the case of La Sayona. Carried away by her own desires, dominated by her animal fury, she attacked her own origin, right in the place that gave her life: her mother's womb. She herself was her own judge, jury, and executioner.

In Latin America, even more so in Venezuela, it is said that "the mother is sacred." Any evil, any sin, any mistake can be redeemed, but the mother figure, being the one that breeds life, is untouchable in every way because it's an offense towards us and towards our history. With this in mind, it can be said that this woman insulted all her ancestors, broke her connection with life itself, condemning herself to live eternally in a liminal space. Ironic that the same happened with her story.

There's a reason behind the saying that "revenge is a dish best served cold." La Sayona is proof of the dangers of not following that creed, of acting in the heat of the moment. No matter what happens, we must keep our heads clear and our hearts calm, lest we make an error impossible to remedy – a lesson I have learned over time.

Journaling prompts

- How do you feel about gossip and rumors?
- Write down one that you are related to (about you, that you shared, or heard); what does it mean? How does it speak about the person it is about? Or how do you feel about it if it's about you?
- What relationship do you have with your maternal family? How have they influenced you? How do you feel about them?

La Dientona: The Dangers of Skepticism

Many times in the past we've heard someone demonstrate their skepticism, believing that this or that is impossible. Sometimes it is even us who believe that we have the last word between what is true and what is not, what's reality and what's fiction, and many times that's why we end up entering the wolf's mouth without knowing it. There's a very particular legend, simple yet direct, that explains the dangers of being skeptical, thinking that *our* reality *is* reality: The legend of La Dientona, The Long-Teeth Woman.

Contrary to the three previous spirits, La Dientona is little known even in Venezuela, but teaches the valuable lesson of not believing that the spiritual world cannot affect the physical. There are two versions of her legend – one that is located in El Tocuyo, Lara, and the other in Tovar, in Mérida.

According to the first version, a man was walking late at night when he found a young, blonde woman who didn't show her face. When he came to ask her about it, she didn't answer, but still – perhaps because he wanted to be a good Samaritan – he asked where she lived. She walked away without looking back, replying, "Soon you will see." It wasn't until they reached a cemetery that the young woman turned around, revealing teeth that looked like knives. "This is my home!" she screamed.

The man ran in terror until he stumbled upon another person whom he had never met. He decided to warn him against the specter from which he had escaped. When he finished telling his story, the stranger asked about the girl's teeth: "Would they be like these?" He had the same teeth, capable of grinding human bones. The man ran relentlessly until he reached his home, safe and sound, and vowed never to go out again at night.

When I was a child, however, I read a different version, much gloomier, located in Tovar. Legend has it that two poets and *serenateros*, serenaders, sometimes named as René and José Jesús, walked through the streets after being at a party. When they found a pretty, blonde girl, she asked them to accompany her to her house.

René suspected that the girl was La Dientona because of her large teeth, and he whispered his suspicions to his friend, but José Jesús didn't believe him, and the girl told them that whispering secrets in front of another person was rude. When they arrived at the house, she asked René to accompany her to the garden to write poems under the moonlight, while she told José Jesús to wait for them in the kitchen.

The hours passed and, tired, he decided to leave, but when he approached to say goodbye, he heard the sound of a dog eating bones. He ran away when he saw that the girl was devouring René's corpse, and invoked La Virgen de la Candelaria while fleeing.

The characters of both versions are in danger by believing that nothing will happen to them. I think it's possible they're the same story, starting in El Tocuyo and ending in Tovar, in addition to the fact that in both versions the specter is that of a blonde girl with sharp teeth who manages to shapeshift, first becoming a man, and then being able to hide her prominent teeth with irregular success.

Many times we venture into the unknown without any precaution, believing that grandma's tales are just that, old stories to scare the children when there really is always some truth in each one of them. When I read the story of La Dientona, I remember a rather bitter episode with the ouija board when I was in high school. Although it was an experience that left me more sensitive towards the dead, something I've used as a therapist more than once, it wasn't a pleasant way to develop this skill.

I also remember all the times when I thought I was prepared, when I overestimated myself and thought I could, and it really wasn't the right time. This happens to us many times, and although experiences leave us with valuable lessons, maybe even a gift, we would have saved ourselves the hard time of having been more prudent and not conceited.

Journaling prompts

- Why would La Dientona live in a cemetery? Maybe cemeteries and skepticism are related or there's some symbolism in it?
- What do you think about death and the dead?
- When was the last time you overestimated yourself? What happened? What did you learn from the experience?

Momoyes: Guardians of Water, Nature, and Justice

When one thinks about the fae – fairies, goblins, and the like – it's easy to imagine them as how they've been pictured since Victorian times, late 19th century England: mischievous, sometimes cruel entities, who are not really interested in working with humans, sometimes with insect like body parts. There are very similar underground creatures in Trujillo.

It is said that momoyes ("moh-*moh*-yes," the plural form of momoy, "Moh-*moh*-ee") lived on the surface when the mountains didn't exist. When the mountains appeared, momoyes decided to live underground, but they didn't separate themselves from the world that was their home just because of that.

According to the legends, momoyes are elf-like creatures that have inhabited the Andean area since pre-Columbian times, especially in the Boconó Municipality. They live mainly in lakes and rivers. They are also known as *mamóes, mumúes,* or water spirits. They are usually described as foot-and-a-half tall little men, with little references to women, with long beards, straw hats, and indigenous clothing, along with ornaments made of feathers, leaves, flowers, and walking sticks.

As for their character, many claim they are mischievous and friendly. However, they also take great care of the environment and retaliate against those who leave waste, pollute, destroy nature in their path, or take something without asking their permission.

There are stories of a momoy who threw a can back at its owner when he left it in a lagoon. Another lives in the Páramo de la Culata, in the state Mérida, who hits campers, especially if they don't respect nature. One's even said to have caused heavy rains in April and May of 2011 when he was captured until he was released, although many claim it is impossible to capture one of these creatures.

They're moderately similar to the fae beings of Celtic folklore, as they like to hide things and play pranks on travelers, enjoy whistling, singing, and dancing, and they have been known to take away black-haired women. It's known that there are some "médicos," Witches who have won their favor and alliance, and these are the only ones capable of undoing their spells when they hex or punish someone. They are also proud, for they disappear if humans ignore their signals, unable to bear being overlooked.

Momoyes seem to be powerful allies of Pagan Witches, but they also carry with them an important lesson about the duality of nature, especially water, the element they're so closely related to. It's easy to imagine guardians of nature as benevolent, friendly, and generous beings, eager to work with us humans, maybe we don't think we're capable of dealing with the consequences of our actions, or maybe we're just lazy, thinking that it's not our responsibility. However, momoyes show us that we'd be wrong in both cases.

Although friendly, these guardians don't hesitate to defend Los Andes, their territory, what's rightfully theirs, and demand their sovereignty to be respected. As such, they are the first to defend their land, to teach humans that they're not just little men with tender faces. Just like water, momoyes are volatile and can change in a second depending on our actions.

Many times, we have allowed ourselves to be invaded, altered, violated, and manipulated by others. It's easy to bow down and nod, and so it takes a storm to bring justice. Many have rocked the world, and many times there's a fair cause involved. Amid racism, homophobia, discrimination, and hatred in all its forms, many have risen up. Water is usually considered the element of healing. It nourishes, cures, and cleanses, but the ocean is not always calm, it's not always peaceful. Sometimes it takes a tidal wave to kill weeds, and I think we all have witnessed it.

Momoyes may be what we understand as elemental spirits. Maybe they're water elementals form Venezuela, something that could be kept in mind when drawing a circle or working with that element. I've been in Trujillo a few times before, always felt a calming, serene atmosphere, and I didn't know it may be because of these spirits. It seems to me that, although fierce when they must be, momoyes are calm and want mortals to fall in love with nature as much as they have. Not only with *outer* nature, but with our *inner* nature as well.

Journaling Prompts

- What's your relationship with water like? How are you similar and different to it?
- How do you heal? What heals you? How would you describe your healing process?
- What are you *by nature*? What feels *natural* to you? Are those things *unnatural* to others? Who's right and who's wrong?
- How would you describe your relationship with nature?

María Lionza: The Venezuelan Queen of Spirits

I discovered magic, spells, rituals, and the whole world of Witchcraft when I was in high school, although I was interested in mythology and legends since I was a child. Every time I entered an esoteric shop, known in Venezuela as perfumerías esotéricas, esoteric perfumeries, almost always there was an image present, a woman with two men. I didn't pay it much attention, but as time went on and as I continued to see her, my curiosity was inevitable. It was María Lionza, the Venezuelan Queen of Spirits.

While I haven't had an experience with her, a close friend of my family has. For matters of privacy, I won't share her name, but as a santera she has worked con la señora, with the lady, as she herself said, and who clarified many doubts and questions about María Lionza.

Who Is This Queen?

According to one version of the legend, Yara was an indigenous princess, daughter of a cacique, an indigenous chief of the region, now the state Yaracauy. She was born sometime during the 15th or 16th century, and was sent to live in the Montaña del Sorte, where an anaconda fell in love with her and devoured her. Terrified, Yara asked the mountain and its spirits for help, so Yara disintegrated and became one with the mountain. Some versions say that the anaconda swelled until it exploded, turning into rain.

Yara became a symbol of freedom, wisdom, and power, and she was chosen as the Queen of the Spirits. She also governs the flora, fauna, and waters. According to some, during the Venezuelan colonial era (approximately 1600-1810), Yara took the name of Santa María de la Onza Talavera del Prato de Nívar, or simply Santa María de la Onza, which was abbreviated to María Lionza. However, this seems like an attempt to convert this indigenous figure to Catholicism.

The Montaña del Sorte, officially named "Cerro María Lionza Natural Monument," is the center of her worship and a sacred place where the main altar to Queen María Lionza is located, and the place where anyone interested in learning about Marialionza must go to be taught. As an estimated 10% and 30% of the national population is devoted to her, the mountain is held in high esteem and respect, to the point that then-President Rómulo Betancourt declared it a monument on March 18, 1960.

The Courts of the Queen

In the cult of María Lionza, also called Espiritismo Marialioncero, Marialioncero Spiritism, she's the figure who presides over all the magical works, rituals, and ceremonies, and to whom offerings are made. She's even called a goddess on some occasions, although it is always emphasized that she's better known as Reina María Lionza.

Her importance lies in that she commands the legions of spirits, known as cortes, courts, and it is she and only she who allows the passage of the spirits to the earthly plane to interact with the living, either through portals or during ceremonies or magical works, where devotees lend their bodies for these entities. In Venezuela, this is called ser materia, to be matter, even if the person is not a devotee of the Queen.

At all times, the image of María Lionza is present in the center of the altar, almost always as a bust, accompanied by two characters: the cacique Guaicaipuro, who fought against the Spanish and leads la Corte Indígena, the Indigenous Court, and Negro Felipe, who fought during the Venezuelan War of Independence, being the leader of la Corte Negra, the Black

Court. The three of them are the most important figures of the cult, and they are known as Las Tres Potencias, The Three Powers, with the Queen always in the middle.

The courts, in a nutshell, are legions of spirits led by a prominent figure who is also at the service of María Lionza, each with a specific objective or "topic," such as la Corte de los Médicos, led by Dr. José Gregorio Hernández; la Corte Libertadora, with Simón Bolívar at its head; la Corte Chamarrera, made up of wise men from the countryside, headed by Don Nicanor Ochoa; la Corte Malandra, a colloquial and very informal word synonymous with criminals, who almost always come from the lower social strata; and la Corte Celestial, la Corte de los Estudiantes, and even la Corte Vikinga.

When one of these spirits enters someone's body, the person acquires their way of speaking and acting as long as the spirit remains in their body, so the identity of the spirit, or at least to which court it belongs, becomes evident. However, the person in question does not retain any memory of the experience, since they enter a kind of deep sleep.

The Pilgrimage

On October 12, Día de la Resistencia Indígena, known as Día de la Raza until 2002, is celebrated in Venezuela. It commemorates the struggles of native indigenous people against Spanish colonizers. On this date, the devotees of María Lionza make a pilgrimage to the Montaña del Sorte in Yaracuy, in the north of the country.

The Queen is honored this day, the curious and willing to participate have the opportunity to do so for the first time, and devotees go into a trance to contact the various spirits, almost always through tobacco, an essential element in practice. This is used for cleaning oneself, cleaning others, cleaning the space, receiving visions, and more.

Tobacco serves as a form of offering, but flowers are much more popular for this use, and they are almost always what devotees leave as a token of respect and gratitude after a request or milagro is fulfilled. The sculpture of María Lionza located on the Francisco Fajardo Highway in Caracas, where she's seen naked on top of a tapir, also usually has floral offerings. Wine is another option that is considered sometimes.

A bóveda is also commonly made. It is a kind of altar that must be mounted on a table; it carries precise elements, and should not be set on the floor. The image of María Lionza is always in the middle, along with Guaicaipuro and Negro Felipe. Bóvedas are also often included when offering a mass, which, contrary to what I originally believed, does include the Catholic-Christian figure of God; the mass itself is directed towards the Queen, though.

The Image of the Queen Today

As a figure, María Lionza is fascinating. Her story is full of feminine empowerment, sacred femininity, and is strongly related to freedom, healing, and justice. Rooted in Venezuela's indigenous beliefs, it also shows the cultural amalgam that characterizes this country.

As I grew up, I heard a lot of comments about her cult and mountain – some positive, but many negative, in which I was told that going to the mountain was dangerous and that it was preferable not to get even close to it. But knowing better the story surrounding Reina María Lionza, what she represents, and her customs, it doesn't seem that harmful anymore.

There are elements I do not identify with, such as the use of tobacco, essential for interaction with spirits and the development of faculties, but the following of the Reina de los Espíritus is still a belief with beautiful values and messages that, in my opinion, Venezuelan society needs so much. Our society can be very prejudiced; it prefers to judge from a comfortable position instead of entering, at least for a moment, the court of a Queen who has even captivated the singers Rubén Blades and Willie Colón – they dedicated her a song with her same name in 1978.

Journaling prompts

- When was the last time you misjudged something or someone?
- Have you been misjudged?
- What kind of spirits do you work with? Do you include those of the land you live in or the one you were raised on?

José Gregorio Hernández: A Five Percent Chance

Those who see my youngest cousin, the smallest of the family, only see a normal girl. She is just your regular elementary school student at first sight. What some don't know is that she had to have more than ten blood transfusions after she was born, and she was helped by a then-folk saint.

My aunt had a fairly uneventful pregnancy. The doctor told her she was worried because the baby wasn't growing enough, but no one in the family paid attention because my aunt is precisely the shortest of the seven siblings and didn't have the typical pregnancy discomforts.

However, as the due date approached and after they decided on my cousin's first name, my aunt began to feel dizzy. She had low blood sugar, aches, pains, and more. It was as if the pregnancy was catching up, but it still seemed like everything would work out, that there was no reason to be nervous.

I was working in a library at the time. On July 21, 2014, my mother called, telling me that they were at the hospital in my hometown, and that my aunt was giving birth, but had the beginning of preeclampsia, a complication during pregnancy where the mother's blood pressure rises more than it should. It could have been fatal to her and the baby. She told me my aunt was already stable, and that we would soon see my cousin. Both were stable, but I learned the details over the next few months, and each one was scarier than the last.

The first thing was that the delivery occurred at eight months, which is fatal for the baby in most cases. Had my cousin been a boy, she would not be alive due to some genetic conditions; girls are still at high risk, though. During those days, my cousin was with the other premature babies. She was the only girl, and there was another empty crib every day.

My aunt's preeclampsia was not "normal," and it got so high that the doctor asked my uncle and my grandmother who they wanted to save, the girl or the mother. There was also the issue of weight and size. Nobody told me that an adult could hold her in with the palm of one hand and that the smallest diaper in the hospital came up to her chest. An adult pinkie was thicker than her arm, and she hardly seemed to have any fat on her body. After various complications, my aunt recovered, but the baby was in intensive care, with a 5% chance of survival. The doctors didn't want to give my family hope, so they said everything in the subtlest way possible, which didn't help much either.

During this time, someone made a family call to Syria, the country where my family comes from. Someone told them that the name they gave her was fatal for the baby due to astrological conditions. They came up with a better one with astrology and numerology, and then everything stabilized.

By then, my cousin had had more than ten blood transfusions, and her parents and my mother had each made a promise. If she survived, my mother would organize a dinner in her honor and would invite the Arab community in my hometown. As for my aunt and uncle, they would take their daughter to visit José Gregorio Hernández, in Isnotú in the state Trujillo. It would be her first long trip, after she stabilized, and everything was over.

Religion Does Not Matter

José Gregorio Hernández Cisneros (October 26, 1865 – June 29, 1919) studied medicine in Caracas, Venezuela, and later in Paris, France, and even wanted to train as a priest, studying in Lucca, Italy. However, it wasn't his studies that made him famous, but that he saw and treated the poor without charging anything, even giving them medicines, until he died when he was hit by a car.

I already knew the story of José Gregorio and that he was an important figure, but when we got to the sanctuary in Isnotú, his hometown, I was surprised to see the number of plaques in gratitude, all after a miracle that the doctor had granted. Entire walls were covered in plaques, flowers everywhere, and a statue stood in the middle of the place, just before the museum in his honor. Such is his fame that he became a folk saint, one of the most important figures in Venezuela. In June of 2020, the Vatican proclaimed him blessed, and it is very possible that he will become the first Venezuelan Catholic saint.

It took a year for my family to recover from this episode and make sure there was nothing to worry about. My cousin began to grow, and with each day she had more energy and her voice became louder. After a year, we went to Isnotú, and my uncle, a faithful believer in the Druze religion, was the one who held his daughter and brought her closer to the statue of José Gregorio Hernández, known in Venezuela as El Médico de los Pobres, "the physician of the poor."

This was, however, my first experience with a figure of another religion. I keep him in mind when I perform reiki therapies, and my mother, eternally in love with our Arabic roots and culture, is a faithful believer in him.

After several years of thinking about it, because I didn't see the point of someone from another religion listening to my family, I understood that, as long as the heart is believing, honest, and respectful, religion does not matter – and also that I will be careful when choosing the names of my children.

Journaling prompts

- What's your relationship with your name? What does it mean? Do you like its meaning?
- Have you prayed or worked with a spirit/entity from a faith/religion/spirituality different to yours?
- Is there a figure that is highly respected in your family? Is there a story behind that respect? Do you share their devotion?

La Loca Luz Caraballo: Losses, Follies, and Family

Ten years ago, when I was in high school, my uncles from France and Syria came to Venezuela. It had been almost 40 years since my father last saw them, and those were days of trips, stories, anecdotes and more trips. In the midst of everything we talked about during a trip to the Andes, I heard the legend of La Loca Luz Caraballo, the madwoman Luz Caraballo.

According to the version I heard, this was a woman with an unbalanced mind who lost her children. She lived during the times of Simón Bolívar, between 1810 and 1823, precisely in Los Andes. She lived near the forests and knew them better than anyone, to the point that she could help anyone who wanted to cross without getting lost.

If I remember correctly, she helped Bolívar himself, and when his enemies, the Spaniards, wanted to find him, she led them the other way. She didn't find rest when she died, however, so it's said she appears in the region.

While looking for more about the legend, I learned that Luz Caraballo is the protagonist of Palabreo de la loca Luz Caraballo, "The Word of the Madwoman Luz Caraballo," a poem by Venezuelan author Andrés Eloy Blanco. Included in his 1959 book La juanbimbada, it tells that Caraballo was a country woman with five children: a daughter who ended up in a seraglio, a brothel; two sons who died; and two more who went after a man on horseback, after which she never saw them again. The latter has been interpreted as a conscription by the army.

These circumstances could certainly have driven many mad – especially women, since Venezuela has always been a macho country in many ways, and mental health is not taken seriously. If something in this story is true, it is easy for me to imagine that a woman could have lost her sanity and, while seeking help, wasn't taken seriously. It's not a very encouraging outlook – gloomy, even.

Eloy Blanco's poem became so popular, along with the figure of Luz Caraballo, that there's a monument for her in Apartaderos, a town in the state Mérida in the Andean region, installed in 1967 by the sculptor Manuel de la Fuente, who ironically was Spanish. On the monument itself there's a bronze plaque that contains the verses along with the image of the author.

Alvio Alfonso Briceño wrote a book, Mi abuela la loca Luz Caraballo, "My Grandmother the Loca Luz Caraballo", in which he claims to be her grandson. In the text, he shares some of her historical information, among which is her real name, María Blasa Rivas, born in 1885 in the town of Jajó, Trujillo state. According to Briceño, Rivas only had two children, a boy and a girl, who didn't want to talk any more about their mother, to the point that the author himself only found out about the relationship in 2004, the year in which he published the book.

Briceño says that the reason for his grandmother's mad walks is unknown, but she would get lost in the Andes and the townsfolk would help her return. At age 42, in 1927, she left her home for the last time, and was never seen again, dead or alive, no matter how much they searched for her. As a result of this, it began to be said that she became a lost soul, and many began to see her as a miraculous spirit to whom they would leave candles and flowers and ask for favors.

She could well have been a new popular saint, although, unlike José Gregorio Hernández, Luz Caraballo was a common woman, not someone famous or credited with a wide-scale impact. However, anyone could see associations and correspondences in the story of María Blasa Rivas, especially in the version I heard in 2010. If she's a spirit of the roads, someone who knows how to move through the Andes, and if she really has granted favors to those who asked, it wouldn't be surprising if we are faced with a nascent belief.

For those interested in establishing a relationship with a spirit that little is known about, partnering is fairly easy. You must carefully read the available material and let the ideas emerge. However, as Briceño's book seems to be discontinued and I have not found a digital copy, I will limit myself to the poem by Eloy Blanco and what I've been able to read about María Blasa Rivas.

Loca Luz Caraballo's connection with travel and movement is undeniable, so I could ask for help in case of being lost, physically and metaphorically. She understands pain and loss, so she could help with healing and emotional catharsis, maybe even with traumatic situations. The love for her family would also make her a guardian of the home, motherhood and children.

Reading her story, it seems like she's someone who had happiness despite everything; she gives me the impression that she's one of those funny grannies who want to lighten the atmosphere and make everyone smile, because they know pain first-hand.

Journaling prompts:

- When was the last time you felt lost, physically or metaphorically speaking? What did you do?
- Is there a relative your family does not speak about? Do you know the reason why?
- Are you comfortable being alone? What does it mean to be alone for you?

Condemned to Loneliness:
Ánima Sola in Venezuela

Venezuela is a strongly Catholic country. Although some Venezuelans are not practitioners, they are often still believers. It's common to hear phrases like "I don't go to church, but I believe in God." This hasn't changed in recent years, and I doubt it will, although I've seen more tolerance and interest towards other beliefs recently. However, this doesn't mean that Catholic figures don't appear in other religions, as in the case of the cortes of María Lionza, or like that of Ánima Sola.

In her book *The Element Encyclopedia of 5000 Spells*, Judika Illes explains that:

> Ánima Sola translates as the "lone soul" or "lonely spirit" and refers to a very specific votive image. Based on Roman Catholic votive statues (but now a standardized chromolithograph), this image is particularly popular in Latin American magical traditions. It depicts a woman standing amidst flames, eternally burning yet never consumed. She gazes upwards, holding her chained hands towards heaven. Is her soul burning in the fire of Hell or does her heart burn with the fire of love? Allegedly unrequited love is what drew this poor soul into her predicament: the Ánima Sola traded eternal salvation for the joys of temporal love. She is invoked in only the most desperate love spells, in which in return for obtaining the sought-after love the appellant agrees to replace Ánima Sola in purgatory when they die.

I heard a different story, however. When I was a teenager, I heard about Ánima Sola many times and was told that she was a condemned soul, a woman punished for all eternity. I've heard several names for her, but it seems the most common is

"Celestina Abdenago." According to legend, this woman was present at the crucifixion of Jesus, and gave drink to Dimas and Gestas, the good and bad thief respectively, but not to Jesus, who condemned her to suffer for all eternity alone for her actions.

Many times I was told that this soul is used to make a person just as lonely as she is, so that their health deteriorates, their plans are not fulfilled, and they suffer in many ways. Although what Illes tells in her book makes sense and I don't rule out the possibility of working with Ánima Sola in a positive way, I have always heard that she's an entity one must be very careful with. Both versions are valid, both are very real possibilities, but the way I grew up has had an impact on me and my way of seeing this legend.

Being a victim of bullying for 11 years, I know what loneliness is. I was suffering from depression, anxiety, stress, among many other things. Loneliness was both a blessing and a curse. Those years were quite strong and changed me in more ways than I first thought.

Loneliness made me want to heal and heal others, especially those like me. I started writing about men's mental health, autism, depression, anxiety, and how to stay in control during an emotional or sensory crisis. I learned reiki, tarot, meditation, and more. However, loneliness taught me that there's a difference between being comfortable being alone and getting used to being alone.

When I hear the story of Ánima Sola, I see a teacher, a woman who knows better than anyone what it is to be on your own, what it is to have no one and to fend for herself. If anyone knows what loneliness is, it would be her.

A then-friend told me that she once saw a Santero tell a girl that she had been cursed with the Ánima Sola and that she needed a strong energetic cleansing. Many bad things had happened to this girl in a short time, her mental and emotional health were already affected. The girl in question improved with the days and she seemed to be calmer as time went by. I don't know the details, but from my point of view, it was a lesson for her to take her place, value herself, and be more independent. Being on your own is a double-edged sword. Ánima Sola is not a spirit to be taken lightly, but she's a powerful teacher too, teaching what no one else knows.

Journaling prompts

- What do you think about yourself? Do you believe it because it was said to you?
- How do you feel being on your own? Are you comfortable being alone or are you used to being alone
- What has loneliness taught you?

El Hachador Perdido: Land and Tradition

Another simple legend with an important lesson, one that a friend shared with me, is that of El Hachador Perdido, "The Lost Ax-man". It's a short and direct story about the power of traditions, especially those that are carried on the earth, those that are related to the place where we are and the respect due to the past, about an enraged soul that punishes those who make the same mistake that condemned him.

Some time ago, this friend told me the story of a man from San Casimiro, in the state Aragua, who went to work on Good Friday and was cursed because of it. The reason for his departure varies depending on the version that is read, but all agree on the general aspects: an ax-man decided to go out to look for firewood in the forest to make his own urn during Good Friday, although custom dictated otherwise for that religious date, and he was punished by his God for eternity to torment those who did the same.

According to what my friend told me, and as I have been able to corroborate in readings and traditional songs, one of the signs that this spirit is near is the constant sound of axes, increasingly loud. The person must pray the Apostles' Creed and turn around on the spot, retracing their steps, to prevent the specter from killing them with his weapon. There's a popular song that speaks of this, "El Hachador", by Cronos:

> *Si por la noche se oye cabalgar algún lamento en San Casimiro*
> *Se pinta la sombra de tu recuerdo,*
> *Si es que te encuentras penando en las montanas del tiempo,*
> *Con gusto hachador perdido, yo te rezare tu Credo.*

If at night a lament is heard riding in San Casimiro,
the shadow of your memory is painted,

if it is that you find yourself grieving in the mountains of time, with pleasure, Hachador Perdido, I will pray your creed.

As I say, it is a short legend, but very direct with regard to its moral: respect the customs and beliefs of the place where we are. It is a sign of humility, and I see it as a way to share in a harmonious way with the spirits of a place, as well as the history that runs under the earth, in the wind, and inhabits its flora and fauna.

When I came to the United States, first staying with relatives in Florida, I started leaving offerings of water to all the powers and entities with which I work: gods, ancestors, guides, and more. For me, it's a way of respecting where I am, of showing my respect.

One time, I was so focused on reading I didn't realize something was hitting the bus. People started throwing themselves to the ground, I was paralyzed, until I heard someone say, "they were shooting at the bus."

There were no dead or harmed people but my life had been on the brink and I didn't even know until several seconds had passed. It was the first time I had experienced something like this, but still I asked myself: "How could I be so irresponsible?" Then I remembered the water offerings, and wanted to cry. I took a deep breath and thanked tirelessly the one or ones – whoever it was – that protected me. After several hours I was able to put the episode behind me and go on with my day to day, but the memory remains alive in my mind.

I know that the power contained in the land, and the traditions that have been carried out in it, is real. I know it was that same power and their guardians that protected me when I didn't know I should do it myself.

Journaling prompts

- Do you pay any respect to the place you live in?
- What do you know about that place?
- Can you think of a time when you were protected? What does it mean to you?

Mujer Mula: When a Woman's Magic Awakens

I'm a person who believes a lot in balance and equality regardless of anything else, but during the month of March there's a lot of talk about the mother, the stepmother, the sister, the daughter, the grandmother, and the figure of the woman in general. There's a legend that speaks very well about the image that the mother figure has in Venezuela and that reminds me of the unique magic that lives in the women of my family.

The legend tells the story of a young woman who worked in a restaurant in Caracas, Venezuela's capital, who once denied a plate of food to her elderly mother and then expelled her from the business.

The grieving woman met a man who gave her a coin marked with the cross of Saint Andrew and told her to go back to her daughter to pay for the plate of food; he also told her not to accept the change from her daughter, but to leave instead and tell her to buy *malojo*.

When she had done what the man told her, her daughter turned into a half-woman, half-mule creature, and so she fled the restaurant. The legend ends by saying that since then the mujer mula, mule woman has appeared in churches praying with a white cloak covering her face.

There are many interesting elements in this story. It's curious that the mother doesn't seem to be married, as we are never told about her husband or the daughter's father; perhaps she could have been widowed. In any case, she is an elderly woman with few resources, if any, who cannot afford a meal.

Then the mysterious man appears who gives her the coin, and not just any coin, but one with the cross of Saint Andrew, which is strongly related to women: he's the patron of old maids, pregnant women, single lay women, unmarried women, and women who wish to become mothers, among other groups of people.

Finally, there's the *malojo* (mahl-OH-ho). This is a word used only in Venezuela, and refers to "a variety of corn or a set of these grass plants or cereals that is only used as fodder or pasture for cavalry or the horse itself and that does not reach a seasoning." (definiciona.com) This suggests that the man, whoever he was, knew what would happen to the daughter after the mother followed his instructions.

This is obviously a legend about ingratitude, respect for the elderly, and even more for the mother herself. In Venezuelan society, it is common for the mother to stay at home with the children while the father goes to work, and there are many traditional and regional songs throughout the country that talk about the mother, sometimes calling her "holy." The fact that a child does not take care of their father would be shocking, but that they don't take care of their mother is inadmissible for any Venezuelan.

This dynamic is not unique to Venezuela. This structure of a mother at home and a working father was repeated in my Arab family to some extent. On my mother's side, my grandmother, aunts, my mother, and more relatives were able to take care of the home and still work regardless of what the Arab community said, always supported by my grandfather, who said that before anything a woman must be able to fend for herself.

I've learned to respect women and men just the same, but my grandma and her daughter all share something: their words become reality, especially if it's my grandma, the matriarch, who's speaking. It takes just their voice to favor change, and it takes my grandma's blessing or disapproval to manifest the impossible. Many stories in my family have shown me so.

Journaling prompts

- What have you inherited from your mom's family?
- Have you explored your feminine side?
- Between your mom's and dad's family, do you think one is more spiritual than the other?

El Silbón and Juan Hilario:
Strength Is in Joining

A few years after writing about El Silbón, and doing some research on the internet, I came across a legend that illustrates very well the teachings of the original myth, along with the dangers of skepticism of La Dientona: the tale of El Silbón and Juan Hilario (*Who*-Anne *Ee*-lah-rio).

According to popular belief, Juan Hilario was a party man and womanizer from the Portuguesa state, in western Venezuela. He went out to party during a stormy night during the month of May, although he was warned not to do so, as the thunder foreshadowed the presence of El Silbón in the area. Hilario scoffed at the legend and left anyway.

As he walked, Hilario heard the characteristic whistle of the specter, but he was sure that it was only his friends who were trying to play a prank on him, so he made fun of them. He also made fun of El Silbón again, who didn't hesitate to show him how real he can be.

Hilario was hit again and again by invisible hands, and although he tried to defend himself as best he could, it seemed that he was rather hitting the air. The attacks did not stop at any time, either, leaving him in increasingly worse condition. It wasn't until friends and neighbors recognized him that they insulted the specter and ordered him to leave. After such an episode, Juan Hilario promised not to go out to party again, much less insult what he did not know.

Although it's true that El Silbón speaks first about the ancestors and reminds us to always honor them and learn from their experiences, Juan Hilario's experience also teaches us that the strength is in the joining. While the poor party animal couldn't stand up to the ghost, a large group did manage to push him away. It's an important reminder that community, bonds, and belonging play an important part in any aspect of one's life, especially when spirituality is involved. This is especially true for Witches, even more for solitary practitioners.

Many times I have been in trouble and I have asked "my people," or "the people from above" as I say collectively, to be with my family and friends. On other occasions, I call everyone and ask them to come with me when I feel like I'm in danger, although I already know that I don't always have to.

Being solitary has its advantages, but the challenges are not few. It requires a lot of confidence, care in where to seek information, and a willingness to accept responsibility for one's actions. It doesn't mean that you have the green light to do whatever you want, but if you do so, you better know how to handle the situation as well.

Today I still want to belong to a group, to experience public rituals, with friends, but I don't need it. Not as before. Coming here to the States meant that I had a few people to rely on, sometimes none, and I had to take care of my family at critical times. I still doubt myself, still need to work on my self-esteem, but for a long time I have noticed that sometimes I'm right. Like Hilario, sometimes I know I'm not as lonely as I think.

Journaling prompts

- Are you comfortable asking for help?
- Who do you ask for if you need it?
- Have you disrespected any spirit or spirits? What did you do to remedy it?

Juan Machete: The Dangers of Impatience

There's a legend that makes me think a lot about the times when, by rushing and not wanting to wait for things to develop in a natural, organic, and calm way, we accelerated the process and ended up with a totally different result than what we were looking for. The story of Juan Machete may be known to some, perhaps not to others, but I for sure will never forget it.

Legend has it that Juan Francisco Ortiz, called "Juan Machete" because he always had one on his belt, wanted to have power, land, fortune, and fame. He was said to live comfortably, not with riches and luxuries, but had a nice life. And this wasn't enough.

Blinded by greed, and evidently without any desire to wait to achieve his goals on his own merit, he decided to speed up the process and make a pact with the Devil. How original, right? And this is where things get scary.

He told him that in exchange for the life of his wife and children, he should take a frog and a hen, to which he should sew their eyes and bury them alive on Good Friday at midnight in a secluded place. Then he should invoke him, saying "Satan" three times. So did the man, and business began to prosper. Juan's name became famous in Los Llanos pretty soon, being synonymous with power, wealth, cattle that did not stop growing, and the envy of everyone around him.

The bliss would not be eternal, however. For a while, Juan Machete saw a black bull with white legs and horns, but he paid no attention to it. It disappeared after a few days, and his business continued to grow, he became a tyrant with the peasants and workers of the region, until after a few years his cattle began to disappear without explanation.

It is said that all the animals were dying from a strange disease, his businesses fell, and a fire devoured his house. Juan

Machete, terrified, hid the chests with money that he had left, before disappearing into the jungle. Some say that his soul still wanders, grieving for his mistakes, and that a man vomits fire in what used to be the lands of Juan so that no one would dare to remove those chests stained with blood.

Details about how Juan treated his workers abound, from baptizing them praying the Apostles' Creed backwards to being a cruel tyrant with whom none could reason. It is a case where power and greed take control of a soul that was previously kind and dreamy, but did not measure the consequences of its actions.

Many times, the Law of Triple Return or the Law of Three is spoken of when the subjects of Paganism and Witchcraft are touched upon. Although it's part of a past in which I became interested in Wicca, I still keep it in mind because it makes sense. Each one reaps what they sow. The fruit will depend on the seed, and nothing born of despair and greed will bring good results. I have seen it in my life, in my family, in my friends, and in the media.

I saw it in the news as well when I wrote the original article, when we were told that we had ten years to save the planet. Meanwhile, I haven't seen an important change to loosen the impact. There are missions to go to Mars, the Moon, and establish space colonies. I can only wonder, instead of that, why not save the colony we have here already? We're at a point where we have to hit the brakes and slow down, or continue in this mindless race and witness the rain of fire.

Journaling prompts

- What happened the last time you lost your patience?
- Have you made a "deal with the Devil" so you wouldn't have to wait?
- Do you do something for the planet?

The Bitter Lessons of
El Encadenado de Michelena

Everyone who knows me knows that I love October – I'm a Halloween fan. Samhain's my favorite holiday, and overall I feel in a better mood during autumn, because the world celebrates the different, the misunderstood, and the unusual. As I look forward to its arrival, when I can enjoy shorter and shorter days and longer and longer nights, my mind wanders to far corners, like the dark streets where El Encadenado de Michelena, Michelena's Chained Man, strolls.

The story of this specter is known in the Michelena municipality, part of the Táchira state, recognized for its many legends. This tells us about a man named José who lived in 1925, good-looking and in love. Although he had a girlfriend named María Eugenia, everyone knew that José was unfaithful to her with various women.

The girl's father, tired of gossip, and probably also feeling shame, decided to settle their accounts. He chased him at night with a club, beat him to death, and asked that the body be left somewhere without ensuring that it would be given a proper burial. This is when everything gets twisted, because José found no rest.

After several days, while the girl's father returned late to his house, he had to go through the front of a cemetery. He remembered his crime and felt a chill run through his body, but kept walking without caring about anything. Later, the spirit of the man appeared to him, telling him that he should pay for his actions.

As soon as he arrived at his home, the man collapsed in terror without anyone understanding anything about what had happened. It is said that he eventually went mad before he died, and although there's no explanation, it is said that it was the same spirit that took his life in revenge.

However, as the years passed, there were many testimonies from citizens of the city about a ghostly figure dressed in a black robe, glowing eyes, and long chains that hung from his arms, crawling through the streets of Michelena. It is said that this figure continues to appear today on the main streets of the town, supposedly from the cemetery to the Santa Rosa neighborhood, during the anniversary of José's death.

I initially remembered the Rule of Three, but there's also a Venezuelan saying that applies to this: "al que obra bien, le va bien". It roughly translates as "he who works well, he does well." For me, it is illogical to expect good things to happen if we're always looking for problems and sowing fury. The same applies if we work honestly, helping others, and trying to carry everything in peace – that is, to be loving and respectable people. This doesn't mean that there aren't exceptions because we're only human, but I don't agree that the ends justify the means. I'm a healer first and foremost, hatred takes endless forms and faces, but there are also some of us who work for a change.

El Encadenado de Michelena is a story that tells us about the consequences of resentment, hatred, of becoming a judge and executioner carried away by anger. This is a powerful feeling: being angry can be the fuel necessary to perform certain works, to train and drain everything that has happened during the day, but it is also a double-edged sword.

I can only think about all the atrocities that could have been avoided if people thought a bit more about the consequences. Like the father and José did in the legend, like we've all done, we are only humans, but we can choose to be *better* humans.

Journaling prompts

- What happens when you get angry?
- Is there an episode involving your anger that you remember? What do you think about it?
- Think about a time when someone was angry with you or about something/someone else. What can you learn from it? Do you see it differently now?

El Pozo del Cura: Mistakes, Wisdom, and Humility

Historically, Samhain has been a date that symbolizes the end of one cycle and the beginning of another, popularly called the Witches' New Year in social networks and in some books. It's a date to leave the past behind and avoid repeating mistakes – something a priest in La Guaira state did not do.

Legend has it that a long time ago there was a shameless priest who lived in the state of La Guaira, near what is now Caruao and Chuspa. The interesting thing about the story is that it tells that this priest used to bathe in a lake in female company, something that went against his religious vows.

His punishment would soon come in the form of death. One day like any other, while the priest bathed without worries, he ended up drowning in the same lake and no one could help him. It is said that his ghost still appears in the lake, now named El Pozo del Cura, the Well of the Priest, reliving his death endlessly, asking for help and lamenting his mistakes.

Everyone makes mistakes throughout their lives. However, as my mother taught me, "it is of humans to make mistakes, but it is of wise people to correct them." I've lost count of the times I've been wrong, every time I had to lower my head, swallow my pride, and admit that I don't know everything or that I had made things worse. But I try to learn from every experience. At the same time, I know that my word has power, that what I represent has power. Contrary to a double-standard priest who broke his word, I always try to keep my promises and make amends for my mistakes.

I had an amazing teacher who taught me how to use rods for divination and therapy, and when she got infected with COVID-19, I asked for her to recover, over and over again, but my mother reminded me that this woman always said to ask for something different: instead of asking for what we want, we should always ask for what is best and most convenient.

I do know that she would have done things a little differently. My maternal grandfather, may he rest in peace, always said that one would reach the end that one was destined for from the day of his birth no matter what, but that the path is up to each one of us. I don't think I have enough power to alter a destiny that might have already been determined, and I have reason to believe that my teacher could have done things differently as well.

Days after, I was remembering the memory of my father, may he rest in peace, and how complicated my relationship with him has always been. However, I know that I wouldn't change anything because what I learned is part of who I am today. The same goes for this teacher.

Many times we want to go back in time, redo our actions, change everything hoping for a better result, but no matter how tempting the idea may be, I always tell myself no, that it's better to move on and not try to save something that is already lost. It's better to learn from mistakes so as not to die in the waters of our own stubbornness.

Years will go by; I will keep making mistakes. I will keep losing special people to me, and remembering their lives. However, I'm also looking to be someone better than that guy they left behind. There are those who leave flowers on their graves but I prefer to tell their stories, apply their teachings, and honor their memory.

Journaling prompts

- What have you learned from someone after they're not here anymore?
- How do you honor their memories?
- What do you want others to remember you for when you're not here?

El Enano de la Catedral: A Legend of Appearance and Deception

As the end of the year approaches, I start to reflect a lot on what I've learned throughout it, as I always do when these dates arrive. I'm proud of how I changed since I came to the United States, especially in 2021. Those were difficult times, but I and my magical senses have grown from my experience of them – rather like the man who met El Enano de la Catedral, the dwarf in the cathedral of Caracas.

The details of the legend change a bit depending on the version that's read – it was even the inspiration for a television special in Venezuela, written and narrated by Óscar Yanes, a famous Venezuelan journalist, chronicler, and writer. However, the general events and themes are maintained in all versions.

Late at night and in total silence, a man was walking close to the city's cathedral in Caracas. It's almost always said that he came from seeing his mistress, his lover; sometimes it's even mentioned that he was a womanizer with an unstable life. He had been warned many times that he should not walk at night, but he continued to do whatever he wanted.

Suddenly, a dog barked near him, causing him to jump in shock and laugh nervously. Upon reaching the cathedral, the man sees a dwarf dressed in colonial clothes who asks for his help to light his cigar. Thinking that he has encountered nothing more than a poor person without resources, the man approaches him without suspecting anything.

Once the dwarf starts smoking, he announces that it's already 12 o'clock midnight, and his body begins to grow uncontrollably until he becomes as tall as the cathedral itself. He then tells the womanizer that, since he likes fire so much, then he will take him to a place where there's real fire. Without waiting for anything else, the man starts running in terror and praying as much as he can, hoping to save himself. When he arrives at his home, he decides it's time to change his lifestyle and stop doubting superstitions.

This, like some other legends I have written about, concerns the dangers of skepticism. It also reminds me of the saying "no todo lo que brilla es oro", translated as "not all that glitters is gold." Just because someone has a friendly face doesn't mean they are to be trusted.

This legend makes me think of relationships, one of them that taught me this the hard way, The first months were a fairy tale, until things changed drastically until it was a nightmare out of hell. Gaslighting, abuse, manipulation, blackmail... and I still wanted that pretty face.

It's something that I've only discussed in depth with my closest friends. It was so much, so devastating, and the damage this person did to me was so big, that this relationship left me destroyed enough that I reverted to suicidal thoughts and self-harm again.

It took me years to finally be able to turn the page, to trust again, to believe again in my judgment and my ideals. Today I feel much better than before: the change is monumental, and those who notice everything in detail see it in me.

"Si el río suena, es porque piedras trae," we say in Venezuela. "If the river sounds, it's because it brings stones." Although we don't know what types of stones there are or how many, it's important to pay attention to what comes to us from other senses. I paid the price for ignoring myself. A pretty face is nice, but I'm looking for a pretty heart.

Journaling prompts

- What would you like to change in your life? Is it possible?
- Have you looked at the bright side of things because it was prettier than reality?
- Would you say you have your head in the clouds or your feet in the ground?

December Suitcases

With the arrival of December, memories also arrive – memories of family, with so many feelings that sometimes they're difficult to express. I would be lying if I said that I always knew that Venezuela is a country full of magic, but its customs are etched in my memory, and one in particular: as soon as December is over, when it's barely midnight and January has only just begun, many take a suitcase and run as far as they can, seeing how far they can travel in the new year. What we didn't know was that even those of us who did not run would leave the country, and we wouldn't have a return date.

Since I was a child, I've always liked myths, legends, and fairy tales, even more so when they are about ghosts, specters, midnight apparitions, and everything similar. Since I was in elementary school, I religiously bought a weekly children's magazine, although eventually I would only read the Venezuelan legends section. Every week, a new specter was added to my collection.

I think it was only during those minutes it took me to read that section that I felt enchanted by Venezuela. I never hid from anyone that I didn't feel good there, that it was not my place, that I wanted to go far, far away – somewhere where I would fit better. It was difficult being the reader kid, the one who analyzed stories and tales in literature class but didn't understand anything about sports. I hated that class, and I hated going to school. I just wanted to come home to read about Egyptian, Greek, and Roman myths, and play something on the internet that had to do with magic.

High school was not much different. I kept reading, I was still lousy at sports, and the bullying got worse every year. Once I was completely alone in a classroom, surrounded by people my age, and no one ever spoke to me. On another occasion, a group of almost 10 guys surrounded me at my chair desk and hit me on the head. A couple of years later, the one who was my best friend turned his back on me.

What made me different became my armor. When I brought a ouija board I had made to the classroom, when I started to draw scars in myself with a pen, when they saw me dressed in black on the streets, when I made drawings inspired by Tim Burton, or when I listened to Marilyn Manson during school masses, others began to fear me. This was my little revenge, to be left alone, but only because I wanted to. Only a few knew that I suffered from depression, anxiety, stress, and suicidal thoughts – and then everyone found out when I arrived with cuts on my hand.

I hit rock bottom more than once in my college years. Even though I had many friends, even though I was a good student, even though I studied in the mornings, worked part-time in the afternoons, studied English at night, did internships on weekends, and in my little free time I wrote for seven digital publications – not counting my books – I felt alone and lost.

I never needed to take a suitcase to tell the universe that I wanted to get away from there. When midnight came and a new year began, I only thought of hugging my parents, my family, and dreaming that the new year would be better. My father left us in 2013 after fighting cancer. But life goes on, and I dedicated myself to being the professional my father always wanted me to be. I finished my studies, I kept my name on the internet, I dedicated myself to fighting for just causes, to educate as best as I could. I started and finished a master's degree, and finally I got a book deal.

It's been almost three years since I finally packed my suitcase. I did not do this because it was January 1, or as a vacation. In the middle of the early morning, with my heart in my throat, red eyes, and as many pieces of myself as could fit in a suitcase and a backpack, I got into a car with two companions and left the residence where I had lived since my birth, leaving behind an entire clan that I miss every night.

After a few days in Colombia in which I didn't know what to think or what to expect, I boarded a plane that took me to Miami, in the United States. My cousins welcomed me there for a few months until it was time to move once again, this time to Utah, much further north, much further away. I lived the first winter of my life while writing the original article, and the third one is about to begin as I edit this book, reflecting on the turns that life takes, so many that I would never end if I counted them all, but I feel calm.

One, Two ... Five Years Later

It's been five years since I published my first article about Witchcraft in Venezuela, five years since I first spoke about my ancestors, and when I look back I can only feel proud of that young boy who simply said "let's see what happens" and sent an email dreaming of writing about Paganism. Five years have passed since I had the opportunity to explore the legends of Venezuela, the magic of its streets, and although I don't like to look back, there's a big part of me that stayed there.

Sometimes we don't have to rush out at midnight to request a ride. In my case, like that of many Venezuelans who now live far from home, something bigger was needed, something stronger. Each story is different, each path is different from the others, and what matters are not those differences, or what made us leave. There are a lot of gaps, a lot of blank spaces in what I just told, mainly for privacy and because I don't think it's necessary to go into my personal reasons, but my life was in danger in Venezuela, and so I had to leave.

The important thing for me is that that child who read about Zeus and Aphrodite while the others played soccer, the adolescent who laughed at the fear of others, the college student desperate to show what he was capable of, and the young adult who dreamed during the day and cried at night: they're all finding peace.

Starting from scratch is not easy. It happened to my grandparents, my uncles, and my father. I'm fortunate to have part of my family here when there are many who are alone, but I can't stop thinking about the faces that I can only see on the phone for now, the hugs and kisses that I miss, the memories that we don't share. The idea that I might not see some of them again. The only thing that motivates me is precisely that, the time I have spent away, and the hope that at some point we will meet again. Meanwhile, I already have experience with suitcases in case I have to move again, ready to be filled with equal amounts of clothes and dreams.

Journaling prompts

- Would you abandon it all to pursue a dream?
- If you look back on your life, what do you see?
- When was the last time you had to move? Why did you do it?

La Loca de Ejido: A Tale of Dependency, Depression, and Healing

There are Venezuelan legends that are easily found, that appear without much searching. However, there are some that take a little more work to find, such as La Loca de Ejido, The Madwoman of Ejido, but that doesn't mean they don't have a particular charm in the best style of gothic novels.

This is one of the few legends that has a clear date: March 26, 1812, Holy Thursday of that year, the day an earthquake in Caracas claimed more than one life. This event affected several cities and states, like Caracas itself, La Guaira, Barquisimeto, San Felipe, and Mérida. It's said that a young man lost his life in this event, and it was the point of origin for a specter whose figure could still be seen in the city of Ejido, Mérida.

According to legend, Lorenzo was a young man who inherited a large fortune after the death of his father. He came from a family with a lot of money, but that wasn't an obstacle for him to fall in love with a humble young woman, Marta.

Both families looked favorably on that relationship, and looked forward to the two lovers' wedding. However, on a trip that Lorenzo had to make to Mérida, the fateful earthquake took place. Marta had to stay in Ejido to take care of her sick mother, while her beloved went with his mother.

Upon hearing the news, Marta went terrified to the capital city. The dead were countless. Tears bathed the ground, cries rose to the sky, and with the passage of time, her despair increased.

They had told each other many times that they wouldn't leave each other. For both her and Lorenzo, it was unthinkable to live separated, and they constantly promised to see each other again soon when they had to go their own ways. Marta kept hoping that this would be another one of those times, but fate would be different.

Death had separated them before their time, since Lorenzo laid lifeless in his mother's arms in the rubble. As they say, from that moment Marta lost her mind. She did not cry, she did not scream, nor did she collapse. But she began to walk without direction and without paying attention to those who called her. Some say that her spirit still wanders through that traumatic vision of her.

It's easy to see that this is a co-dependent love story where both members feel they're worthless without the other. However, it also talks about the most crushing kind of depression a person can experience. Is it possible to die from a broken heart, from depression? Not long ago I heard about a case where an older man died of depression after so many deaths from COVID-19, including that of a good friend, my cousin's grandfather. I also know of the case of a mother "dead in life" after the murder of her son. The heart seems to be the strongest organ in the body, capable of recovering many times. But it is also the most fragile, obliterated when it receives certain blows.

My practice as a Witch began to focus on healing because that was exactly what I needed. It was what made me most desperate, that emptiness in my chest that ate me from the inside without warning. Not knowing what to do with my own pain, I did my best to become a counselor for my friends and family, learned to put myself in the place of others, and use my energy to ask for their well-being.

At the beginning of 2022, a good friend told me that he realized that he has a "very nice healing power." "I'm developing it and it makes me feel very peaceful," he told me.

"The most destroyed will always be the best healers," I replied. "We're the ones who best know what it is like to be down." That phrase has stayed with me, and I think it will for a long time.

A healer knows hell firsthand, and that's where their power comes from. Contrary to La Loca de Ejido, the healer knows how to use their pain, learn from it, and grow as an agent of change. That's precisely what makes us so dangerous: we know how to find the wound and close it to get up and raise our kindred.

Some people look at me funny when I say that I practice Witchcraft, that my main interest is to heal, help others, and help myself, but that's the least of it. I know my specters, my demons. While I haven't tamed them all, there are several that bow their heads to me.

Journaling prompts

- When was the last time you felt depressed? Why was it?
- Write the names of your personal demons. What do they represent? How can/could you exorcize them? There's power in naming things, so do you thinkm you could name them to tame them?
- Of those demons, which can you control? Which ones have you taken the power from?

Healing with the Venezuelan Flag

It doesn't bother me to think about the past. I quite like it. It shows me what I've done, what I've achieved, what I need to get better at, and I have a lot of good memories to keep myself motivated. Looking back at that boy who didn't feel he could ever fit in in Venezuela, the young man who was in danger and resented all of Venezuela, I came to think about a healing exercise: healing with the flag of that same country.

They taught me at school that the Venezuelan flag is composed of three colors with a profound meaning: yellow, for the rich land and resources; blue, for the Caribbean Sea; and red, for the spilled blood in the path to independence. It also has seven stars, representing the seven signatories to the Venezuelan declaration of independence. It currently has eight according to the government, but we who oppose the government don't use that version.

I started thinking, "what if that same flag could be the base for a healing method?" I kept thinking and came up with the idea of meditating with those same meanings. For me, meditation is writing, so I worked the concept as writing prompts, but it could be adopted into other forms.

Yellow: What Makes Us Rich?

I'm obviously not talking about money, wealth, or possessions. What makes someone unique? What is it that makes you be *you*? It can be a characteristic, an ability, a talent, an interest, a dream, a way of doing things, the work a person does... What enriches us as individuals?

I was told that my maternal grandfather, may he rest in peace, used to say that Venezuela is, or was, a paradise. Comparing it with Syria, he used to say that it was a blessing to have every kind of weather, every kind of food, the whole year, and that

71

Venezuelans were kind and polite all the time. He also used to say that Venezuelans don't know what they have, how lucky they are to be in such a country.

Remembering that, I like to wonder what it is that makes me different from all others. It's easy to say we are all different, but in reality, how are we?

Blue: What Makes Us Free?

It's an interesting question because, one, it builds on the previous one, and two, because we take our uniqueness for granted, while we may actually be adopting thoughts, feelings, and even actions that are not our own. We can learn and adapt, but are we being honest with ourselves? Are we our true selves?

I don't need to remind myself what I want to do for the rest of my life. I know it already, and I've known since I was 13 years old, but I've heard many times, from people my age, younger, and older, that they don't have a single idea. My first question is always the same: "What do you like to do the most?"

Being honest, what does your real self enjoy? If you know it, keep doing it, do it better, and stay loyal to that. That's my definition of freedom.

Red: What Makes Us Strong?

I don't like the idea of fears being prisons. They can certainly become such, but I look at them as opportunities for shadow work. Coming from an immigrant family, and being an immigrant myself, I was told a lot of stories of how all of my relatives, even my parents, had to face different fears. I had to do it as well. Be it in Syria, Venezuela, the United States, or another country, we had to take a deep breath and go on.

One of my grandfathers had to go to school with sandals in the middle of winter; my dad slept in the cold streets of Polonia; my mom raised my brother and I after dad died; and I had to be there for my brother when he got an emergency surgery when we were still new in the United States, him not knowing enough English and having a hearing deficiency. We come from a lineage that doesn't stop because of fear. We give each other strength in the middle of distress.

How do we find our own strength when we need it the most? How do we face fear? How do we stay free?

Seven Stars: Seven Wishes

A few years ago, in 2017, I remembered something I learned from Tim Burton's *Alice in Wonderland*. They said something about listing impossibilities, things that seemed too crazy to become real. But then what if we worked hard enough to achieve them? Who is anyone to say this or that is impossible?

I listed a lot of dreams, crazy ideas, until I had nine. Nine dreams, nine wishes, and I've made them real so far, although, as I write this, I'm still working on the sixth.

That's what I've told some of my friends and relatives to do: list those goals, those dreams, put them in the right order, from the easiest to the hardest, and commit ourselves to make them real. How hard can it be? The year has 365 days, and every four years you get an extra day. That's more than enough time to plan, act, work, and conquer. Veni, Vedi, Veci.

Planning and making all this inner working is easy, but going toward those dreams is the actual work, and it's the point in all this. Dreams change, evolve, and they may not be just as you planned them to be at some point, but the essence remains. I'm not the same person I was in 2017, and I expect the same to happen when I look back in 10 years, but my dream will stay the same: I still want to be a full-time writer.

Five Years Looking Back

It's ironic that, coming from a family of immigrants, a descendant of people who left Syria in search of a better future and fleeing the collapse and danger they faced in that country, I find myself in the same situation, leaving a whole life behind and starting from scratch in more ways than one. The most ironic thing for me, however, is that Venezuela has been a constant source of inspiration for five years. Without realizing it, I have written and learned about Venezuelan folklore more than any other. I know stories that I had never been told, good friends shared others with me, and I have seen my family from different points of view. I only now realize how much I have grown, and while I don't see myself settled in Venezuela right now, I can tell that it looks different from a distance.

Five Years Ago

I searched for that first email I sent applying to be a book reviewer, reliving the frustrations I was experiencing at the time, the dreams that were about to materialize, and everything that living in Venezuela meant for me, only to be left speechless. I was such a different person at that time.

I wasn't sure about my image, what I could and couldn't say about myself, how honest I could be, and despite my fears I'm happy I took that step. I was never afraid to send proposals or knock on doors. To paraphrase a famous author, what's the worst that could happen? If I got turned down then I looked for another opportunity, but being a part of a team, writing a column every month, has been more than just that. It has been an experience.

As interesting as the legends of other countries were, those of Venezuela were the ones that caught me, the ones that stayed with me, the stories that accompanied me for years. Those myths were the ones that made me understand the country where I grew up in a better way, the ones that made me see my family with different eyes, find the magic in my lineage and the land that saw me grow up.

Looking back, although as a child I loved the stories of the Greek gods, although my mother told me about the Egyptian myths, although in my adolescence I leaned towards the Celts, I found my place among La Llorona, El Silbón, Momoyes, Juan Hilario, El Hachador Perdido, María Lionza, La Sayona, and many more. I looked outside what I found inside without even planning it.

As far as my spiritual practice is concerned, I don't worship Venezuelan spirits, I don't follow a traditional Witchcraft lineage, but I understand myself better and my practice has changed after analyzing those myths and their symbolism. I did some introspection work with each of them that I couldn't do with other stories, and although there will still be some that I don't know, those that I can recite without problems have become special to me.

All of this is ironic because I never felt a special interest in anything Latin in general, and now that I'm away and have a different perspective on things, I look back with a certain nostalgia. Time does not pass in vain; I have known this since I was a child and listened to the stories of my parents and grandparents, who knew what it was like to be hungry and taught me to eat until the last bite. I grew up surrounded by stories, the weight of the years, the memories that are built over time, to form my own.

I really wanted to walk around the country, visit the places of these legends, live an experience worth telling. However, going back to Venezuela is not an option for me at the moment. But I'm still writing this story, and I hope that by the time it ends, it is worth telling.

Journaling prompts

- What do you see when you look five years back in your life? How have you changed?
- What do you expect to see in five years from now? Where do you think you will be in your life?
- What has pushed you forward in times of need?

La Mula Maneada: Corruption, Hate, and Forgiveness

I struggled with life for several months as I finished this book, I had problems connecting with everything, couldn't find peace, and tried to find my way back to my core. I had so many personal issues that without realizing it they took me over. Shortly after that, I found a legend that, although sad, had a message I loved: La Mula Maneada, the Hobbled Mule.

It is said that a woman who lived during the colonial era, although without specifying the exact place, Ramona Esqueda, had a private mule. She had trained it to kick and was using it to unfairly punish the workers she had. It's said that the kicks of the mule were even lethal.

Over time, the mule became so dangerous that its owner had to *manear* it. *Manear* is a word that means "to tie the animal's legs." This is done so it doesn't move, usually to milk them or do anything else. However, the peace would be short-lived.

The Venezuelan War of Independence broke out on April 19, 1810, and the ranch was burned down. All the animals managed to escape, except for the mule. When the war ended, on November 10, 1823, the peasants sought to recover their crops, but eventually they saw a creature that caused havoc: a ghost mule that breathed fire.

What was once a dangerous animal was now a beast from hell. The curious thing about all this is that I didn't find anything about a protection, a prayer, an offering, or anything that appeases the mule. It seems that hatred is stronger than anything else in this case.

My first thought upon reading about this specter was the spiritual symbolism of the mule. In this, the website, Diffen, was quite helpful:

A mule is the offspring of a male donkey (called a jack) and a female horse (called a mare). Mules inherit desirable qualities from both donkeys and horses; from the horse they inherit strength and stamina, and like donkeys, mules are generally patient, sure-footed, intelligent and have an even temper. Mules are sterile but female mules are known to produce milk.

Reading about the donkey and the horse as spirit animals was also helpful. Basically, the mule is a hybrid that combines the responsibility and cunning of the donkey with the freedom and endurance of the horse. It's a wise spirit that can help so much, and one person went to the trouble of corrupting it.

Evidently it wasn't a matter of one day to break the noble character of a creature like the mule. I'm sure Ramona Esqueda had to work day and night to turn it into a violent animal, capable of kicking so dangerously that she herself would end up fearing it.

As I said before, the legend does not mention any protection, and I think that speaks volumes about the message of the story itself. Sometimes the danger is too great, the risk is too high, and it's better to stand back. Sometimes it's better to save yourself the fight – we can't always be the superheroes.

This has been a difficult lesson to learn. Since I was a child I always despised violence. Bullying turned me into a pacifist, preferring words over blows. I've taken several hits in my life, but I've never felt comfortable about it. I've gone through beautiful moments, but also difficult situations that brought me to the brink of madness, and I lost my way.

During this time, I lost a close friend I thought I could always count on, but our relationship changed so much that, when I told her how I felt about it, she decided to end everything. It hurt, but it would have been worse to keep going like that. Distance was a bittersweet solution, but a necessary one, nonetheless. We can't always save things. It was a decision I learned to respect from day one. Meanwhile, I smiled when I remembered her. Contrary to the mule, I've learned to deal with the hatred of others, but also to take distance when I see this.

Although I lost a very special person, I realized it was for the best, that I'm better off without her, and she without me. I learned to stop my own fire and to recognize when someone isn't willing to do the same. I had to distance myself so as not to get hurt more than I already was, something the peasants will surely do when they see the mule spitting fire.

This same friend apologized after some time, after both of us had their space and time to heal and made amends. It was a reminder that, sometimes, goodbyes are just temporary. And then, it happened again. She insulted me, disrespected me, invalidated my emotions, started gaslighting me, and as much as I asked her to stop and just let things be, she kept going on.

I simply wished her well, blocked her, and when she messaged me on Instagram, I blocked her without responding. Although it hurt, it healed way faster than the first time, just in minutes, because I knew I didn't do anything wrong, and because I focused on the good memories. That's more important to me than how she decided to end things. Now, I just get a sad smile when I think of her.

Sometimes, goodbyes are temporary. Other times, they are for the best. And that's perfectly fine.

Journaling prompts

- When was the last time you put some distance between yourself and someone else?
- How do you feel when putting a limit?
- Have you put limits to yourself? Were they for the best?

The Tears of La Llorona: A Tarot Spread for Mental Health

At the end of 2023's Spring, I fell asleep with a panic attack and woke up with suicidal thoughts. I'd been going through a very difficult few weeks. So many personal situations that have been coming together, unresolved traumas, and emotions I hadn't been able to express, that have brought me to the brink of collapse.

I've been in therapy for months, and at that point in time I started suffering from panic attacks. Two to three times a week, I lost control of my body, my mind, everything that it meant to be me, until I fell into despair. To those who haven't had it, I hope they don't experience it, and to those who know what they are like, I hope they never go through it again.

At one point, my therapist told me that if this kept going, with such recurring attacks, he'll have to refer me to a psychiatrist. That was at the beginning of the week. A couple of days later, I lost control again: I went back to that state of mind where I didn't care, where nothing made sense, where nothing was worth the effort I put in. Where I just wanted to give up.

I reacted, but soon after I had the second crisis that left me exhausted and unstable for the rest of the day. I told myself: "If it's time to go to a psychiatrist, so be it." But I've never wanted to depend on medicines – I didn't want to feel weak. So, it occurred to me to ask for help from "the people from above."

It had been a long time since I read cards to myself, and yet my first thought was, "I'm going to do a tarot reading." The sketch of the spread came to mind instantly. I made a few changes, a few last-minute tweaks, but after trying it out, I knew I'd be using Las Lágrimas de la Llorona, The Tears of La Llorona, again.

Why that name? Because I hadn't stopped crying every time I could, wondering what will become of me, what I was going to do, what I could expect, what I should change. I remembered the legend of La Llorona, and that ended up shaping the decision when I was at my job. I tried it as soon as I got home and just as expected, it clarified many things for me.

How to Do It

This is a general reading about our perception of life and how we feel about it, quite an illuminating experiment. For this reason, I suggest that the reader try not to be with anyone when they try it. It is an emotional, private, and very personal moment.

To do it, form three columns of four cards. The first, on the left, represents the past. The second, on the right, is the present. The third and last is the future. The first card in each column is the eye, our way of seeing things. The second card in each column is memories, the ones that we create, are creating, and that we could create. The third is how we have or are going to evolve as a result of it. The fourth card in each column is the result: those for the first and second columns go to the sides, while the middle one is straight all the way.

Finally, the last card is placed on top of all the others, crowning everything and representing guidance, revelation, learning, and so on – any word works, although for me it's the divine words regarding reading.

For quick reference, here's the list:

Eye of the past
Memories from the past
Evolution from the past
Results from the past
Eye of the present
Memories being created in the present
Evolution from the present
Results of the present
Eye of the future
Expectations regarding the future
Evolution in the wake of the future
Possible results of the future
Divine word

I trust that it will serve others as much as it did me. It's not a substitute for the therapy that I've been receiving or the one that I may receive, but a form of support to have a better image of my situation, to make conscious some unconscious or repressed ideas, and to serve as a meditation to be able to move forward.

Conclusion

Working on that column for so many years, and now on this book, remembering all those moments, learning about myself, my legacy, my heritage, making amends with my past and what I've gone through, has been more healing than I expected. I never saw myself writing about Venezuela, even less celebrating it.

Looking back, I can only see that lonely boy who cried every night, cutting himself as he thought about giving up on life, I smile as I tell him "we did it". We are safe, we're on the right track, we're free, we're happy, and we're alive. Even though life was terrifying, even though we became our own worst enemies, we did it.

I don't know when it happened. I don't know when I started to change so much. There's not a moment I can point at and say "here" or a memory that ignited it all. Somewhere along the way, I started wreaking the cage, and I can no longer imagine myself in it.

The spirits and legends of Venezuela not only offer teachings and morals, symbolism and magic. They are witnesses of a change. Both my personal change and that of a whole country many had to run away from in order to survive. I've changed in front of them, a collection of creatures that taught me a lot along the way.

My bittersweet relationship with Venezuela changed for the better. I can't go back, it's not safe for me for several reasons, and I guess it will be a long time before I can go visit. However, the man that will do it will be different from the guy who left. He'll be more thankful, more connected to the land that raised him and shaped him in many ways, and will know more about the magic that waits in the Llanos, Los Andes, the forests and jungles.

In the end, it was its legends who made me appreciate Venezuela, the same legends that have seen me change and evolve as a writer, a Witch, and a human being. I'm proud of what I've done and what I've learned so far, and that's all that matters.

I can only hope that you do, too. That you allow the legends of your lands, or your ancestors' land, to teach you and guide you in this journey. They might look foreign at first, but there's a home in there waiting for you.

And it's great to find it.

MOON BOOKS
PAGANISM & SHAMANISM

What is Paganism? A religion, a spirituality, an alternative belief system, nature worship? You can find support for all these definitions (and many more) in dictionaries, encyclopaedias, and text books of religion, but subscribe to any one and the truth will evade you. Above all Paganism is a creative pursuit, an encounter with reality, an exploration of meaning and an expression of the soul. Druids, Heathens, Wiccans and others, all contribute their insights and literary riches to the Pagan tradition. Moon Books invites you to begin or to deepen your own encounter, right here, right now.

If you have enjoyed this book, why not tell other readers by posting a review on your preferred book site.

Readers of ebooks can buy or view any of these bestsellers by clicking on the live link in the title. Most titles are published in paperback and as an ebook. Paperbacks are available in traditional bookshops. Both print and ebook formats are available online.

Find more titles and sign up to our readers' newsletter www.collectiveinkbooks.com/paganism

For video content, author interviews and more, please subscribe to our YouTube channel.

MoonBooksPublishing

Follow us on social media for book news, promotions and more:

Facebook: Moon Books

Instagram: @MoonBooksCI

X: @MoonBooksCI

TikTok: @MoonBooksCI